Fun and Games with the Recorder

by Gudrun Heyens and Gerhard Engel
Translated and adapted by Peter Bowman

Method for the Alto Recorder

Tutor book **1**

ED 12703

www.schott-music.com

Mainz · London · Madrid · New York · Paris · Prague · Tokyo · Toronto

ED 12703

British Library Cataloguing-in-Publication Data.
A catalogue record for this book is available from the British Library.

ISMN M-2201-2257-6
ISBN 1-902455-13-4

Cover illustration John Minnion
Text illustrations Julie Beech, John Minnion
Design Peter Klein
Music setting Jack Thompson

Foreword

Dear Parents and Teachers,

Fun and Games with the Recorder is a tutor for soprano and alto recorder which comprehensively covers all stages from the beginner's first notes through to in-depth work with advanced players.

This **Method for Alto Recorder**, which is a continuation of the three volumes for soprano recorder, will continue to place great importance on developing musicianship, breathing technique, sound production, rhythmic security and the introduction of music theory.
At the heart of this method lies a seamless crossover from soprano to alto recorder whilst maintaining and developing the student's soprano recorder playing. It is not necessary for students beginning this method to have worked with the earlier volumes of the series but it is essential to have some knowledge of the soprano recorder.

The first volumes of **Fun and Games with the Recorder** for soprano recorder are intended for use with children from about six years of age. This method for alto recorder is therefore aimed at children of around 10–12 years. As in the previous books in this series we address the child directly and provide carefully planned and precisely formulated exercises.

This method is suitable for use both in group and individual lessons. In order to encourage and develop group music-making the accompanying **Tune Books** offer a broad range of solo and ensemble music which is graded to match the technical and musical progression of the **Tutor Books**.

The **Teacher's Commentary** explains all aspects of the tutor as well as offering additional suggestions for consolidation of contemporary playing techniques, intonation, breathing, articulation and alternative and trill fingerings.

We wish users of this tutor every success and happiness with their recorder playing.

Gudrun Heyens and Gerhard Engel

T = refer to the **Tune Book**

C = refer to the **Teacher's Commentary**

Contents

From Soprano to Alto Recorder

Hello!
Gather around with your soprano and alto recorders and introduce yourselves by
playing to one another.

What is the difference between the soprano and alto recorder?

The soprano recorder, also called descant recorder, is a recorder in C
because its lowest note is a C.

The alto recorder, also called treble recorder,
is a recorder in F because its
lowest note is an F.

1 Dance and sing

Dance and sing and jump a - round, we love to hear the mu - sic sound.

Practise this song on your soprano recorder until you can play it from memory.
Note: throughout this book   S = soprano recorder   A = alto recorder
The first note is a **g.** How do you finger this note on the alto recorder?
With the first note of the song securely in your mind pick up your alto recorder and play the song again beginning
on the same note.

This is the fingering we use to begin the song on the soprano recorder:

When we want to play the
song on the alto recorder
we finger the g like this:

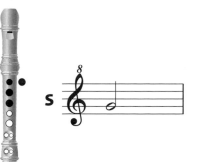

You will hear that both fingerings produce the same note.
Compare your soprano and alto recorders once again.

Notice that:
For the soprano recorder the notes are written an octave lower than they sound.
To show this a little number *8* is written on top of the G-clef.

Find out the fingerings for the following notes and complete the fingering charts yourself.

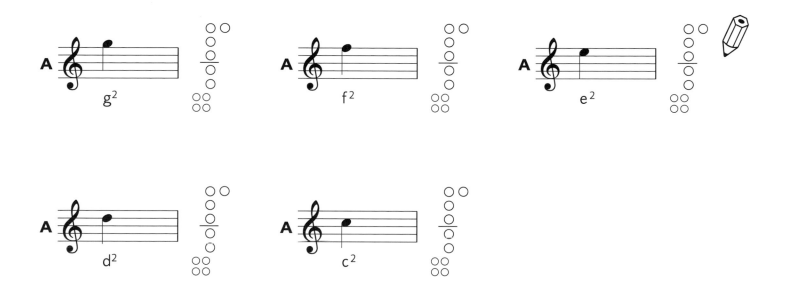

Now you can write out the song for the alto recorder and play it both on the alto and the soprano recorder.

Songs using 5 notes (c–g)

Play these songs first on the soprano recorder and then on the alto recorder. Write out the song for the alto recorder.

2 Creeping up the staircase

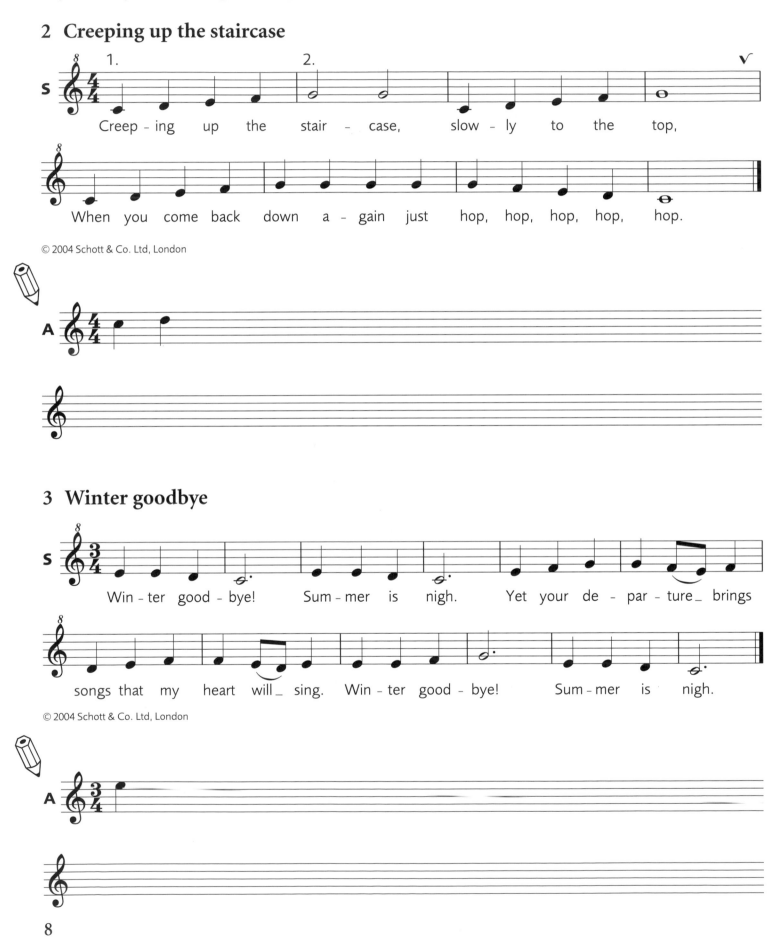

Creep - ing up the stair - case, slow - ly to the top,

When you come back down a - gain just hop, hop, hop, hop, hop.

© 2004 Schott & Co. Ltd, London

3 Winter goodbye

Win - ter good - bye! Sum - mer is nigh. Yet your de - par - ture_ brings

songs that my heart will_ sing. Win - ter good - bye! Sum - mer is nigh.

© 2004 Schott & Co. Ltd, London

4 Song of the Eskimos

FINE

At-te kat-te nu-wa, at-te kat-te nu-wa, e-mi sa-de mi-sa-du-la mi-sa de.

He-xa ko-la mi-sa woa-te, he-xa ko-la mi-sa woa-te.

D. C. al Fine

A

5 C'est le roi Dagobert

S

C'est le roi Da-go-bert qui met sa cu-lotte à l'en-vers.____

vers.____ Le grand Saint E-loi lui dit: O, mon roi, vot-re ma-jes-té est mal

cu-lot-tée! C'est vrai lui dit le roi, je vais la re-mettre à l'en-droit.____

A

Two melodies

Warm-up exercise for tune 6.

6

G. Engel

Write the missing slurs in the alto recorder part.

G. Engel

7

G. Engel

Tunes 6 and 7 fit well together. Play them one after the other to build an A-B-A-Form.
Finish by repeating tune 6.

8 Echo game for soprano and alto recorder

Listen, play, then write it down

Remember:
The little *8* on top of the clef shows that the soprano
recorder sounds an octave higher than it is written.

G. Heyens

9 For tuning

Add the following rhythmic accompaniment:

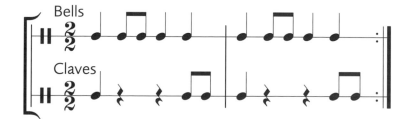

10 Happy duo

G. Engel

T There are more duets on pages 4 and 5 of the **Tune Book**.

An exercise for holding the recorder C

Hold your alto recorder so that it rests on your lower lip and is supported by both thumbs.
Your fingers should hover 1cm–2cm above the holes.

What can you do to make the recorder feel more secure in your hands?

Now that you have found a secure holding position try moving your head and arms without
dropping the recorder.

Finger exercise

Slap the three fingers of your left hand noisily on their holes.
Experiment with all possible finger combinations.
Finally, include your left thumb in the exercise.

Try this short exercise using the fingering for f-sharp:

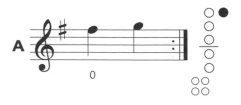

Exercises for balance using 5 notes

Warm-up Exercise: Gently stroke the left hand finger-holes to ensure that there is no tension in your fingers and wrist. Practise the notes under the brackets to ensure that your holding position is well balanced.

11

G. Heyens

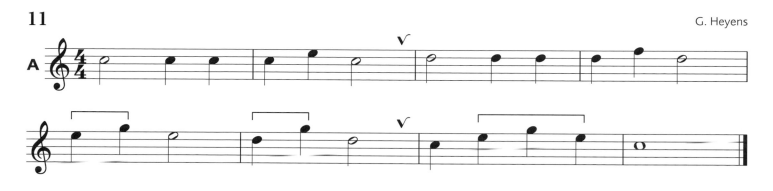

12

13

14 Try playing this exercise with the eighth notes slurred in pairs.

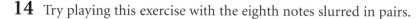

Finger gymnastics C

Your fingers are used to the soprano recorder.
What is different about the alto recorder?
Compare the weight and size of the two instruments, the distances between the finger holes
and how they feel in your hands.

Play your soprano and alto recorders and notice how far your fingers have to stretch in order
to cover the holes of the alto recorder properly.

Now play the following finger exercises on both instruments. Think about how the two
instruments feel under your fingers.

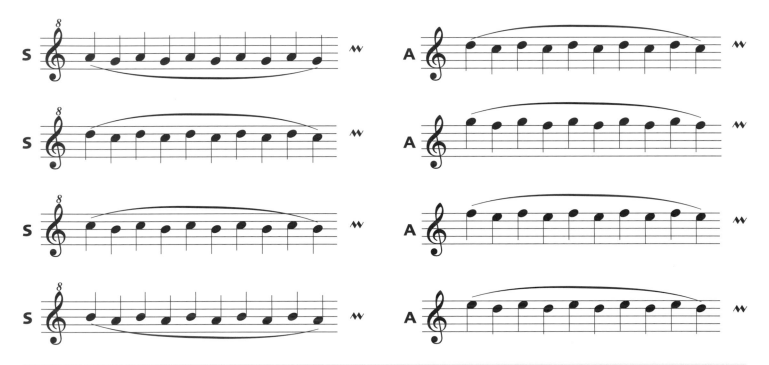

14

15 The Night

Allegretto

G. Engel

Think about how you can play pieces 15–20 with the appropriate character: which tempo would you use? Which kind of articulation? Think up your own title for no. 19.

ritardando (**rit.**) = becoming slower
a tempo = at the original speed
dolce = sweetly, gently, singing

16 Birds on the wing

Play freely

G. Engel

T There are pieces to play with piano on pages 4 and 5 of the **Tune book**.

17 Lullaby

G. Engel

Count: 1   2 and 3

$\boldsymbol{f}$ = *forte* = loud (strong) $\boldsymbol{p}$ = *piano* = soft (weak)

$\boldsymbol{mf}$ = *mezzo forte* = moderately loud

18 Dreaming

for soprano recorder ...

G. Engel

and for alto recorder ...

G. Engel

19 Two altos – five notes

A dotted eighth note and a sixteenth note together equals one quarter note:

G. Engel

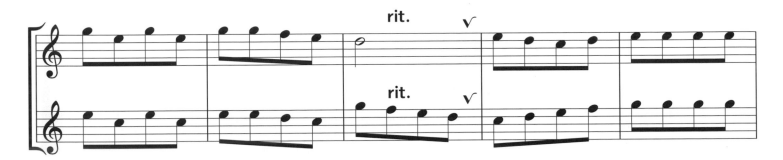

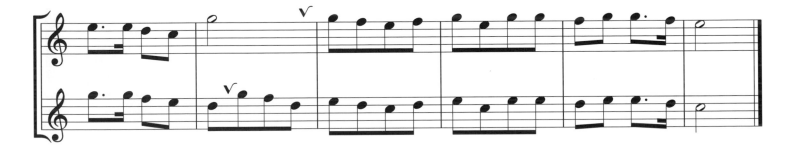

20 The happy alarm

G. Engel

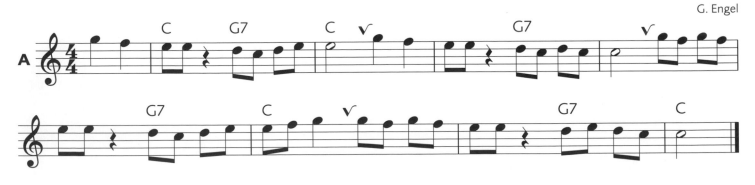

21 Minuet

Anon.
(ca. 1700)

22 Minuet

Esprit-Philippe Chédeville
(1696–1762)

Teacher

From: *Französische Tänze für 2 Blockflöten (S oder A)*, Schott ED 41404

Minuet: a graceful dance, very popular during the 17th and 18th centuries.

23 Canario

Joachim von dem Hofe
(1612)

Accompaniment:

compose your own accompaniment:

Triangle
Xylophone
(Soprano recorders)

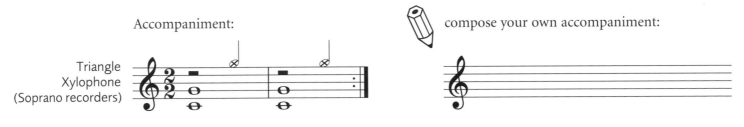

Canario: a lively partner-dance very popular in the 17th and 18th centuries, especially in France.

24 Gavotte

James Hook
(1746–1827)

From: Hook, *Easy Duets*, Schott ED 8878

Gavotte: an old line-dance with a skipping step still danced in parts of France.

High C

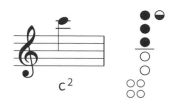

c^2

Two finger exercises C

Beginning from low c (c^1), find high c. Take a deep breath and smoothly alternate between low c and high c.
Only your thumb should move, stopping at the position where the high c sounds best.

Remember: when opening the thumb-hole keep your thumb loose and relaxed. Use a gentle stroking action with
the end joint of your thumb and open only a small gap at the top of the hole: ●

In the following exercise use the rests to make the thumb movement:

25 The Yodeller

G. Engel

Count 𝅗𝅥. (one beat per bar)

Yodel: A type of folk singing
popular in the alps.

26 Triad echo

G. Heyens

T There are more tunes on pages 6 and 7 of the **Tune Book.**

Breathing exercise

With your soprano recorder, take a deep breath and carefully walk across the room while playing a low g. Stop when you run out of breath and make a note of how far you walked. Go back to your starting point and with your alto recorder play the same g as you walk across the room again. How far was your journey this time? What is the difference in the amount of breath used by your soprano and alto recorders.

27 C

Play this tune first on the soprano and then on the alto recorder.
Play the piece at exactly the same tempo both times and mark in your breath marks using a different colour
for each version. Begin on the soprano recorder with bottom c.

G. H.

28 What shall we do this evening?

Jacob van Eyck
(1590–1657)
Setting: G. H.

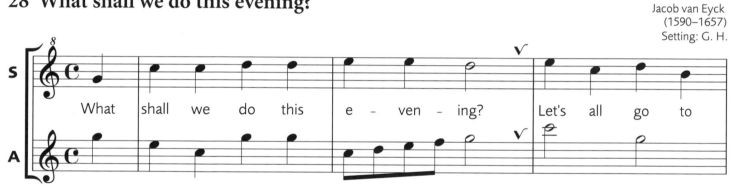

What shall we do this e – ven – ing? Let's all go to

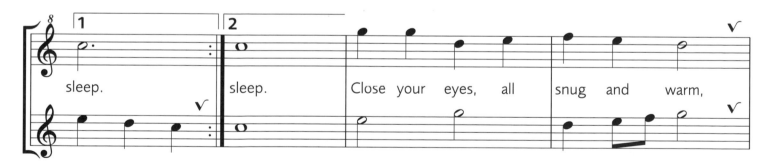

sleep.   sleep.   Close your eyes, all snug and warm,

Sweet dreams com – fort 'til the morn.   Let's all go to sleep.

24

29 Party time C

A listening game

We wish you a mer-ry Christ-mas, we wish you a mer-ry Christ-mas, we

wish you a mer-ry Christ-mas and a hap-py New Year.

Should auld ac-quain-tance be for-got for the sake of auld lang syne. I'll

drink a cup of kind-ness yet, for the sake of auld lang syne.

Hap-py birth-day to you, hap-py birth-day to you, hap-py

birth-day dear ... ... Hap-py birth-day to you.

T Find ways of producing the following sounds:

Doorbell

S + A Chatter of the guests

p

Sounds from the kitchen

S + A Laughter

S + A Excited voices as the food is passed around

mf ———————————— *f* ———————— *staccato*

A Spitting out the cherry stones

A + Tenor Adult voices

Can you think of any more ideas?
Remember that the atmosphere at the party is noisy and happy. The three songs can be heard all mixed up with the other party sounds.

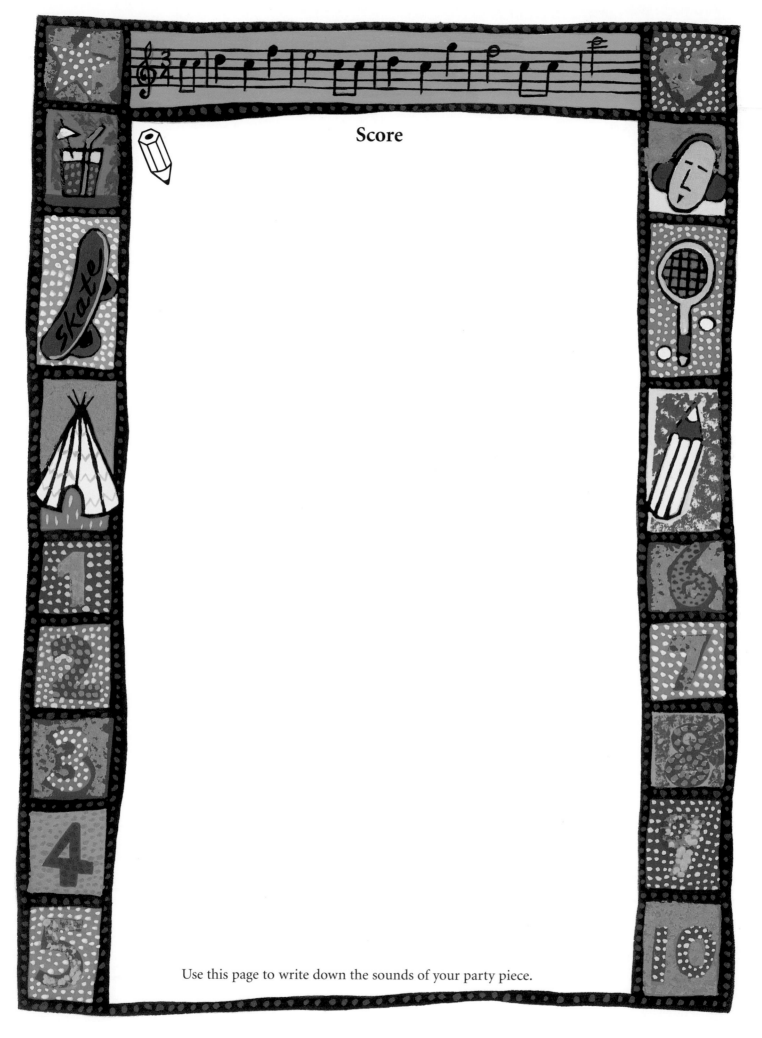

Score

Use this page to write down the sounds of your party piece.

High and low A

Echo game

For the echo game we have included two new notes.
Work out the fingerings for high and low a yourself and then fill in the fingering charts below.

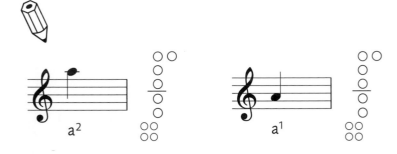

3 Finger exercises for high and low A

30

G. Heyens

31

32

G. Heyens

T There are more high a²s to play in tunes 8 and 9 in the **Tune Book**.

33 Two exercises for intonation C

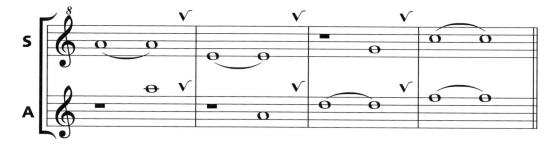

34

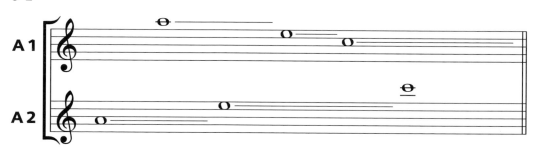

35 Minni Amor

Spanish
16th century

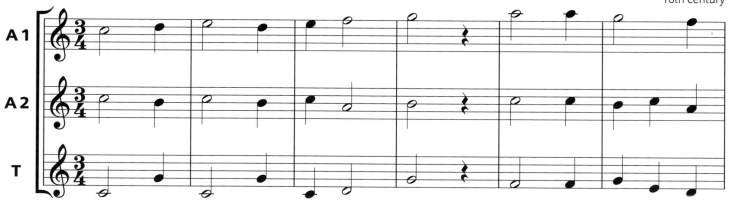

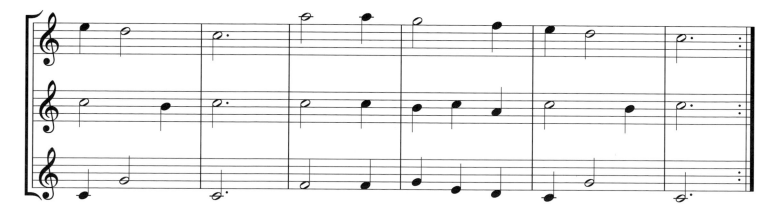

From: *The Recorder Book*, Schott ED 11380

36 Catalonian dance

Anonymous
Setting: G. H.

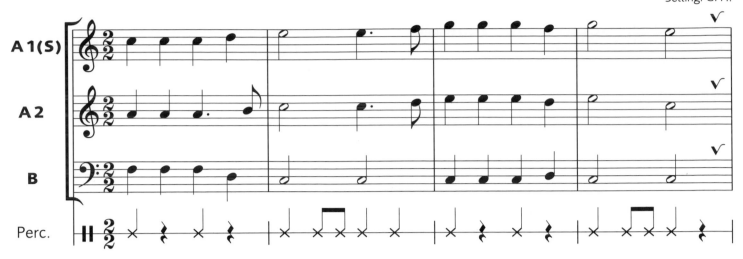

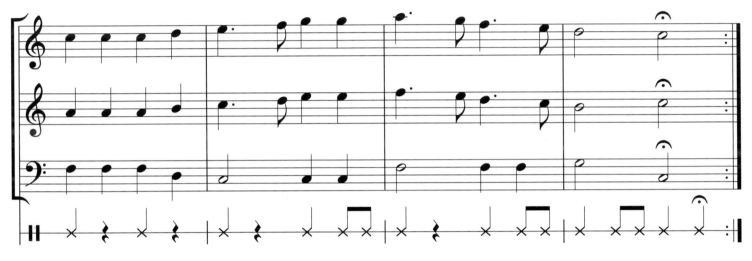

37 Kumbaya my Lord

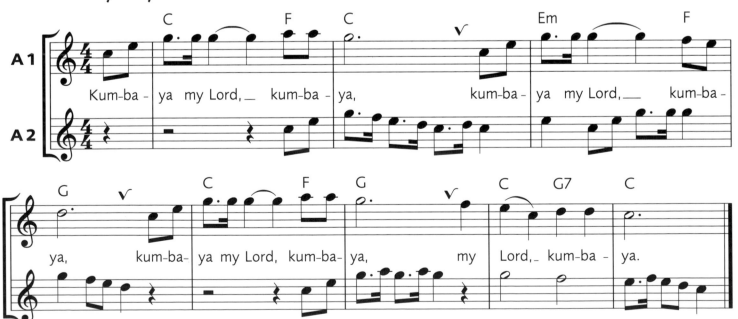

Kum-ba- ya my Lord,__ kum-ba- ya, kum-ba- ya my Lord,__ kum-ba-

ya, kum-ba- ya my Lord, kum-ba- ya, my Lord,__ kum-ba - ya.

The top line of 'Kumbaya, my Lord' can also be played on the soprano recorder.

Articulation: do   to - do   to

Playing dotted eighth notes:

38 Lotus blossom

from China

A

Tonguing exercise

For the piece 'Hunting Tune' we need to use a lively, bouncy articulation.

Practise the articulations on one note: (play - whisper - play)

to-do, to-do, to-do, (as in 'what are we going to do today')

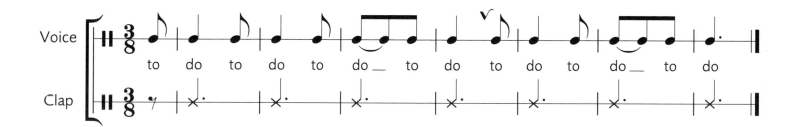

Voice

to do to do to do __ to do to do to do __ to do

Clap

39 Hunting tune

Setting: F. J. Giesbert

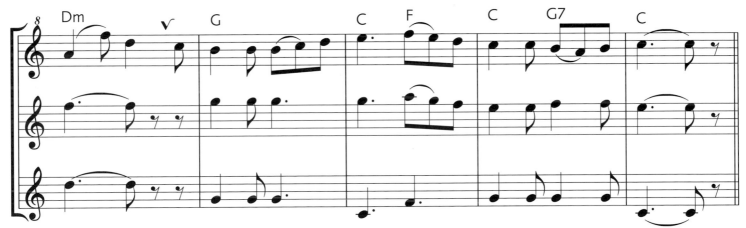

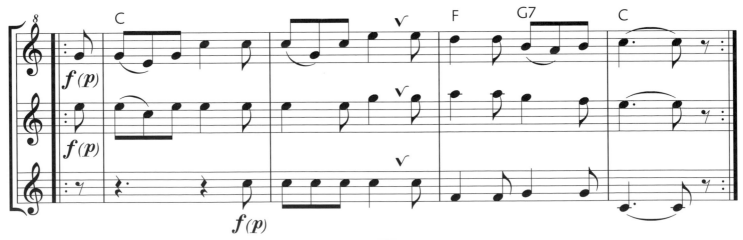

T There are more tunes on pages 8 and 9 of the **Tune Book.**

Breathing exercise C

Stand with your legs apart and let the upper part of your body and arms flop forward so that your head and arms hang down between your legs; put your alto recorder to your mouth and slowly breathe in, 'sucking' the air in through the recorder as you slowly stand upright. Make sure that breath and body have the same tempo.
When you are standing upright play a long note. The air should flow out of you completely naturally - you may even be able to hear your heartbeat in the note. How do your tummy muscles feel? Do you feel comfortable and relaxed?

Do the exercise again using only the head of the recorder but this time breathe out in one big puff as though you were panting after heavy exercise ('phhhhh' or 'ufffff'). At the end of the tone you should be able to hear a very quiet, short single note. What note is it?

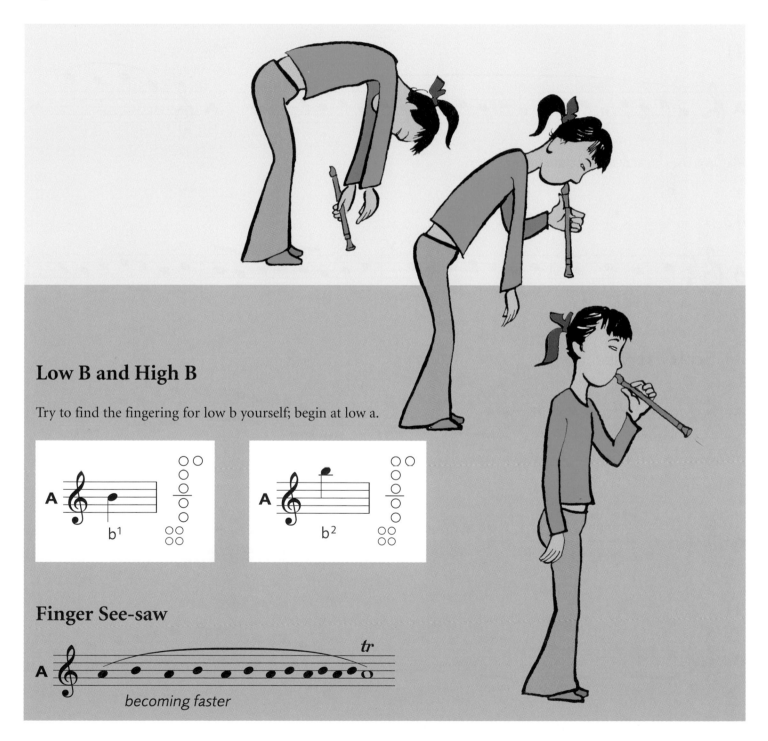

Low B and High B

Try to find the fingering for low b yourself; begin at low a.

b¹

b²

Finger See-saw

tr

becoming faster

33

Exercises C

Take a deep breath and play each exercise until you run out of air.

40

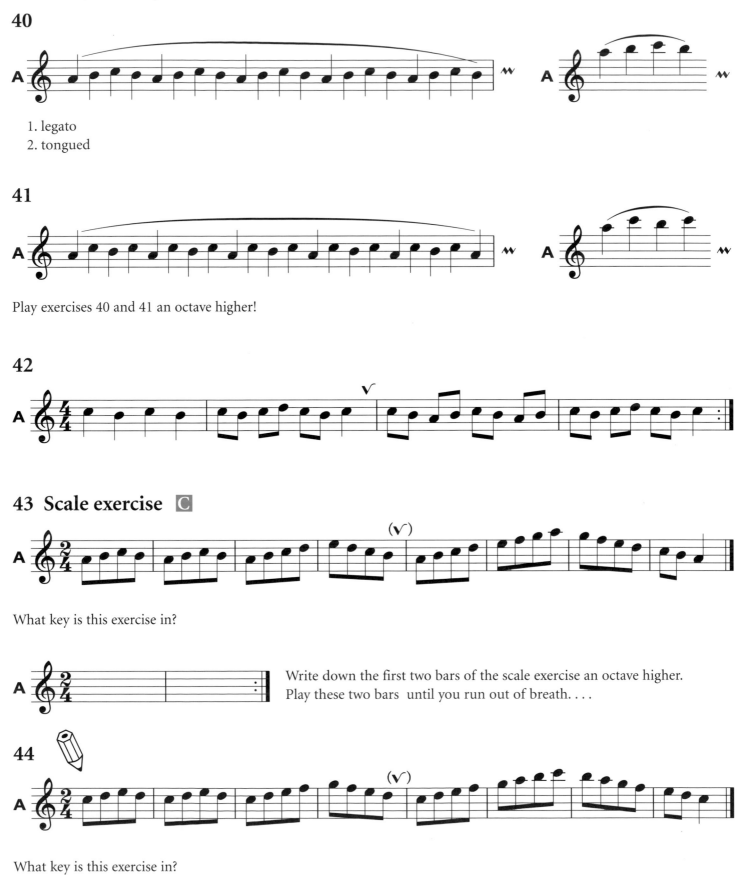

1. legato
2. tongued

41

Play exercises 40 and 41 an octave higher!

42

43 Scale exercise C

What key is this exercise in?

Write down the first two bars of the scale exercise an octave higher.
Play these two bars until you run out of breath. . . .

44

What key is this exercise in?
Mark the semitones in exercises 43 and 44 then learn to play both exercises from memory.

Revision of high notes on the soprano recorder

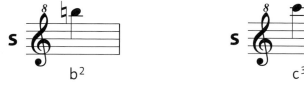

45 Arpeggio exercise C

Tip: Whisper first then play on a single note:

    ‖: <u>do</u> do do | <u>do</u> do do :‖   ‖: <u>do</u> do do do | <u>do</u> do do do :‖

Try it with the syllable "to":

    ‖: <u>to</u> to to | <u>to</u> to to :‖   ‖: <u>to</u> to to to | <u>to</u> to to to :‖

Combine both syllables:

    ‖: <u>do</u> to to | <u>do</u> to to :‖   ‖: <u>do</u> to to to | <u>do</u> to to to :‖

46 Gavotte

Giovanni Mossi
(1690–1750)

47 Polish dance

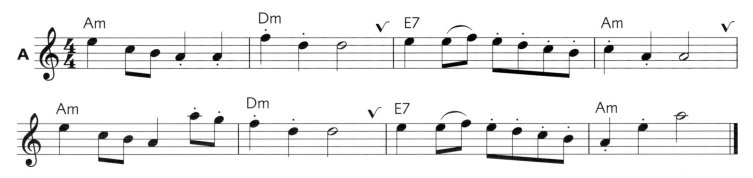

48 Evening mood

49 Holiday happiness

Compose your own tune. See if your friends can guess what you were thinking of.

50 Swanee River

American folk song
Setting: G. Heyens

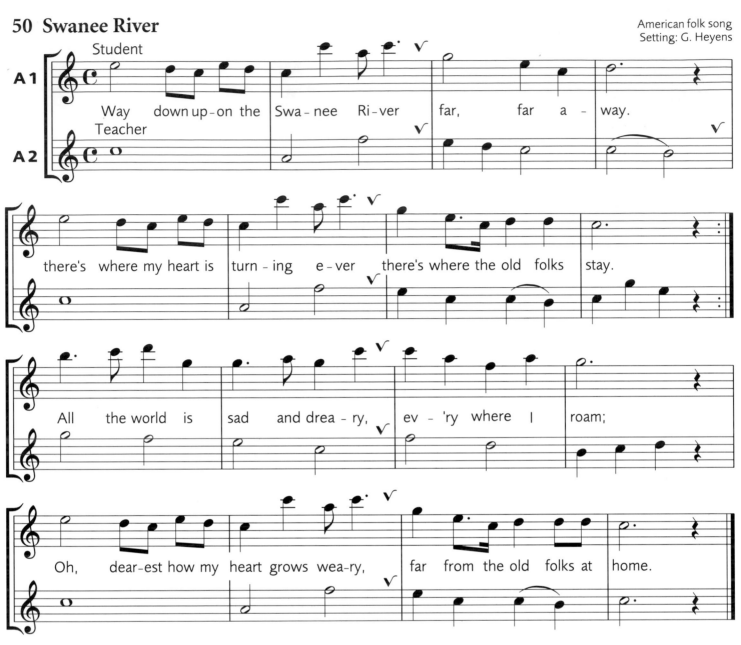

Student

A 1

Way down up-on the Swa-nee Ri-ver far, far a - way.

Teacher

A 2

there's where my heart is turn - ing e - ver there's where the old folks stay.

All the world is sad and drea - ry, ev - 'ry where I roam;

Oh, dear-est how my heart grows wea-ry, far from the old folks at home.

© 2004 Schott & Co. Ltd, London

51 A tune for the parrot

A

From: *The Bird Fancyer's Delight*, Schott ED 10442

38

Syncopation C

52

Have we already learned this piece?*

'Slovakian Dance' will sound really lively if the first quaver of each bar is played short.
* Fun and Games with the Recorder, Tutor Book 2, page 38.

Rhythm game C

Walk around the room at a moderate tempo. For each step clap once and sing do-do-do-do…

53

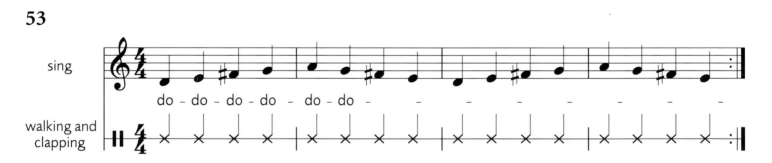

This time begin the tune with a short note (d) so that the second note of the tune has already begun before the second step (and clap) begin. This displacement continues until just before the end when another short note (an e) is added to bring the rhythmical swing to an end.

54

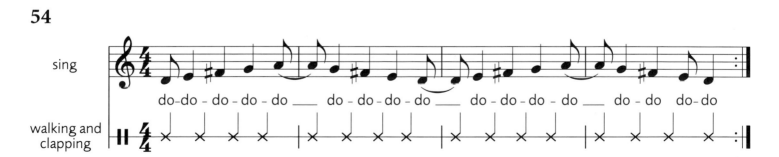

First, sing and clap the displaced tune. When you can do that really well walk around the room as you sing and clap. Finally, step and clap together with the tune displaced.

55 A little syncopation

Johannes Runge

Now it gets a little more complicated!

56 Rhythmic study

Hans-Martin Linde
(b. 1930)

Note: this displacement of the stress is called syncopation.

57 Rhythm swing

G. Engel

T See 'Syncopation Duet'
on page 14 of the
Tune Book.

Study = exercise piece, ètude

58 Linstead Market

Jamaican folk song

A

Perc.

Car-ry me ack - ie go a Lin-stead mar-ket, Not a quat - tie would sell.

Car-ry me ack - ie go a Lin-stead mar-ket, Not a quat - tie would sell.

Lord, not a mite, not a bite, What a Sat - ur-day night.

Lord, not a mite, not a bite, What a Sat - ur-day night.

59 Intonation exercises C

For two alto recorders

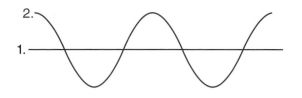

For two soprano recorders

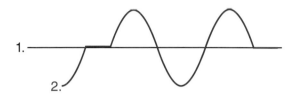
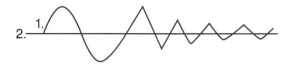

For one soprano and one alto recorder

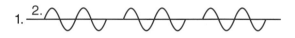

60 Duo for good ears C

Play the following piece slowly, listen carefully and take care to play in tune.

G. Heyens

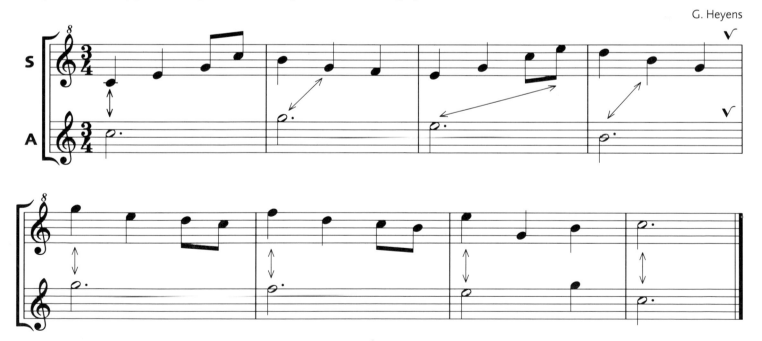

You will find a duet for soprano and alto on page 7 of the **Tune Book**

61 Hunting the hare

Freda Dinn

From: Freda Dinn, *My Recorder Tune Book*, Schott ED 10077-01

How are you going to articulate in this tune?
Think back to 'Hunting Tune' on page 32.

Allegro = fast, lively   **Unisono** = when several voices play together at the same pitch or in octaves

Low C sharp

Try to find the fingering for low c sharp yourself; begin at low d.
Does it sound higher or lower?

Finger See-saw

Finger exercises C

62

63

64

65 Allemande

Tilman Susato
(1535)

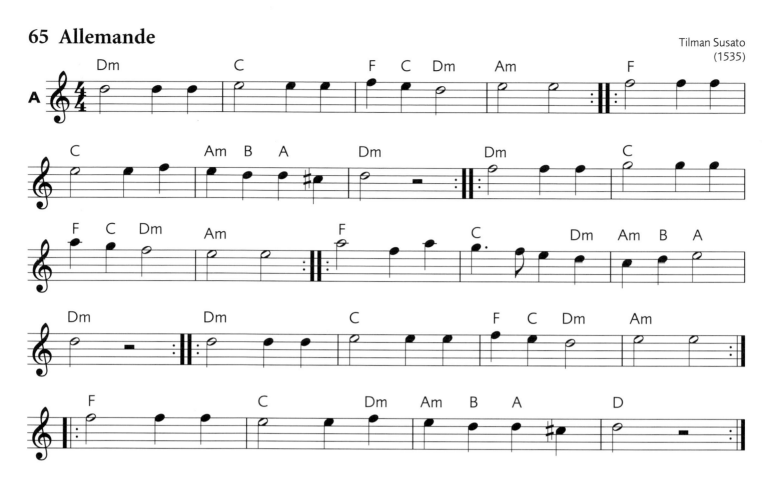

From: *Alte Tanzstücke für Altblöckflöte und Gitarre*, Schott ED 2660

Allemande: A German dance in moderate tempo which was very popular during Renaissance and Baroque times.

66 Folk song

Setting: G. H.

67 Spiritual

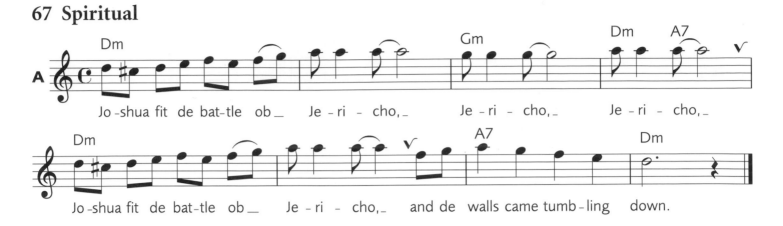

Jo-shua fit de bat-tle ob _ Je - ri - cho, _ Je - ri - cho, _ Je - ri - cho, _

Jo -shua fit de bat-tle ob _ Je - ri - cho, _ and de walls came tumb -ling down.

Spiritual: a religious song of the African-American people.

The First Ornaments

'Trills add brilliance to music and are essential.'
(J. J. Quantz, 1752, famous flutist and teacher
to Frederick the Great, King of Prussia)

Two exercises for trilling [C]

68

Note: In Baroque music, trills at the end of pieces or sections nearly always begin on the note above.

69 Minuet

Monsieur Naudot
(1730)

A 1

A 2

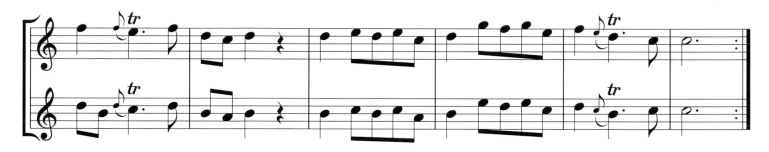

From: *Französische Tänze für 2 Blockflöten*, Schott ED 4104

70 Rigaudon

Jean Hotteterre
(ca.1700)
adapted P. C. B.

A

Adapted from *The Rustic Wedding* (Ed. F. J. Giesbert), Schott ED 2431

Rigaudon: an ancient Provençal dance in lively duple time

Short Trills (Mordents)

The **lower mordent** 〰 begins on the main note
and consists of one 'beat' to the note below.

The **upper mordent** 〰 begins on the main note
and consists of one 'beat' to the note above.

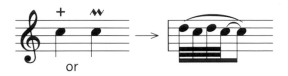

The **short trill** + or 〰, like the longer trill, begins
on the note above but consists of two 'beats'.
Short trills are played mainly during the middle of a piece.

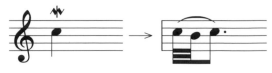

Don't add the trills to 'Ariette' until you know the tune well and can play the rhythm accurately.

70 Ariette

Jacques Aubert
(1689–1753)

From: *Französische Tänze für 2 Blockflöten (S or A)*, Schott ED 4104

Ariette: 'short song'

 Note: Composers often used the sign + to indicate a trill. The sort of trill we play depends
upon the character and tempo of the music and the length of the note you are trilling.

Try to play this piece with all the trills. Check with the trill chart if you are in doubt about which fingerings to use.

71 Brunette

J. B. de Boismortier
(1682–1765)

Tendrement (tenderly)

From: *The Delightful Companion*, Schott OFB 16

Brunette: A type of song popular in France during the 17th and 18th centuries. The songs often refer to young brunettes and the main character is that of tenderness.

72 Air

Robert Carr
(1686)

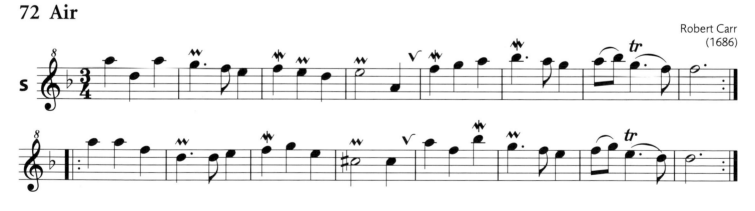

© 2004 Schott & Co. Ltd, London

Air: A piece which is like a song or has the character of a song.

The trill is just one of many ways of ornamenting a tune.
The Pavana 'La Cornetta' contains variations of the tune, these are also 'decorations'.
You can play the decorated version for the repeat.

73 Pavana 'La Cornetta'

Anon.

Pavana (It)/Pavane (Fr): A slow and stately dance

Drum
accompaniment

52

Listen - Play - Improvise

Echo game   C

All stand in a circle. Your teacher will play two whole notes which you take turns to copy. A steady quarter note beat should be felt throughout the game and can be provided by one student quietly tapping a hand-drum or tambourine. The teacher will begin the next round without a break; listen and play.

Try to think up more variations, remembering to ornament only the first bar and making sure that it always has four beats.

Note memory

The teacher (or one of the students) calls out a note name; one student plays the note on the alto recorder, another writes it on the board. Take the game a step further by having the first student also play the note on the soprano recorder and then writing it down in soprano notation.

These are the notes we have learned so far on the alto recorder:

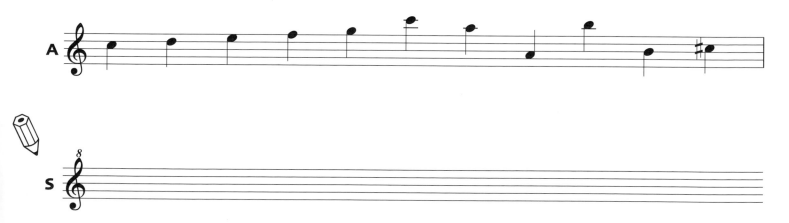

74 Me and my friends C

A listening game for two alto and one soprano recorder.

Discuss together a situation that you would like to 'play', for example: a group of friends are gathered together in the playground during break…etc. Agree the contents of your piece, including details of all the musical building blocks, and then put them together to make a piece of music. It could, for example, be in the form of a 'conversation'.

Write out a score.

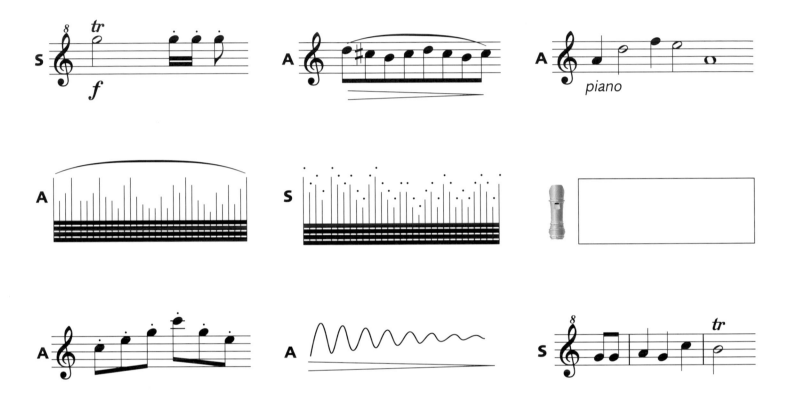

Interrupt the 'conversation' sections with 'singing' sections consisting of beautiful tunes. The tunes can be played more slowly and repeated several times:

What is your piece about?

Are you having an argument?
Are you making fun of someone?
Are you having a serious discussion
or are you just being silly?

Write your score on this page.

Low and high b flat

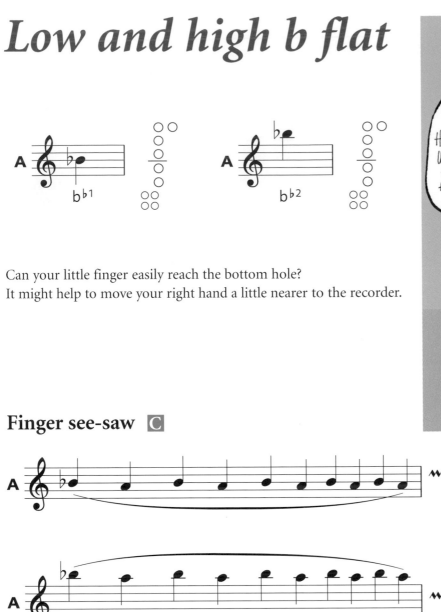

Can your little finger easily reach the bottom hole?
It might help to move your right hand a little nearer to the recorder.

Finger see-saw C

Exercises for B flat[1] and B flat[2]

Use your right hand fingers as drumsticks. By slapping your fingers on the holes you can make a 'drumming' noise.

75

76

77

G. H.

78

79 Sad melody

Calm tempo

G. H.

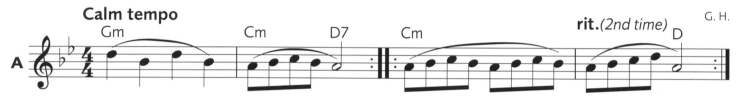

A guitar accompaniment would suit this piece.

80 Silent oh Moyle

From: Freda Dinn, *A Systematic Method for Treble Recorder*, Schott ED 10079

T There are more tunes with b flat on pages 13 and 14 of the **Tune Book**.

81 Greensleeves

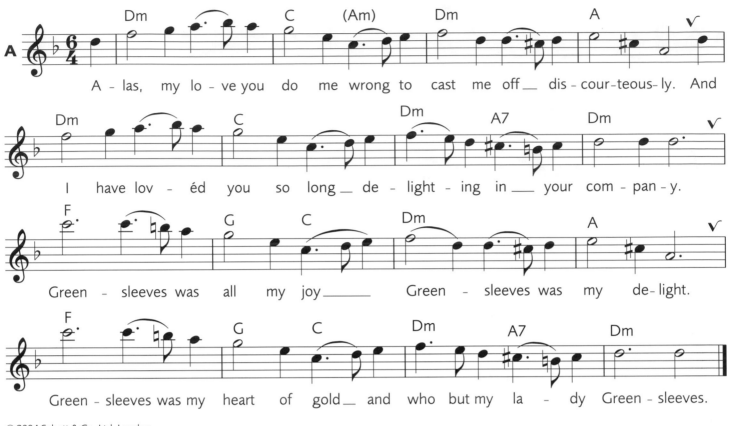

A - las, my lo - ve you do me wrong to cast me off __ dis - cour - teous - ly. And

I have lov - éd you so long __ de - light - ing in __ your com - pan - y.

Green - sleeves was all my joy _____ Green - sleeves was my de - light.

Green - sleeves was my heart of gold __ and who but my la - dy Green - sleeves.

82 Allegro

From: A Solo by Mr. Deane

Allegro

* For low g see p. 72

From: *The Flute Master, Selected Pieces for Solo Alto Recorder*, Schott ED 6605

83 Canon 'Of honest malt'

Richard Brown
(d. 1710)

T See pages 16 and 17 of the **Tune Book**.

84 Air

Anon.

85 Adagio C

Anon.

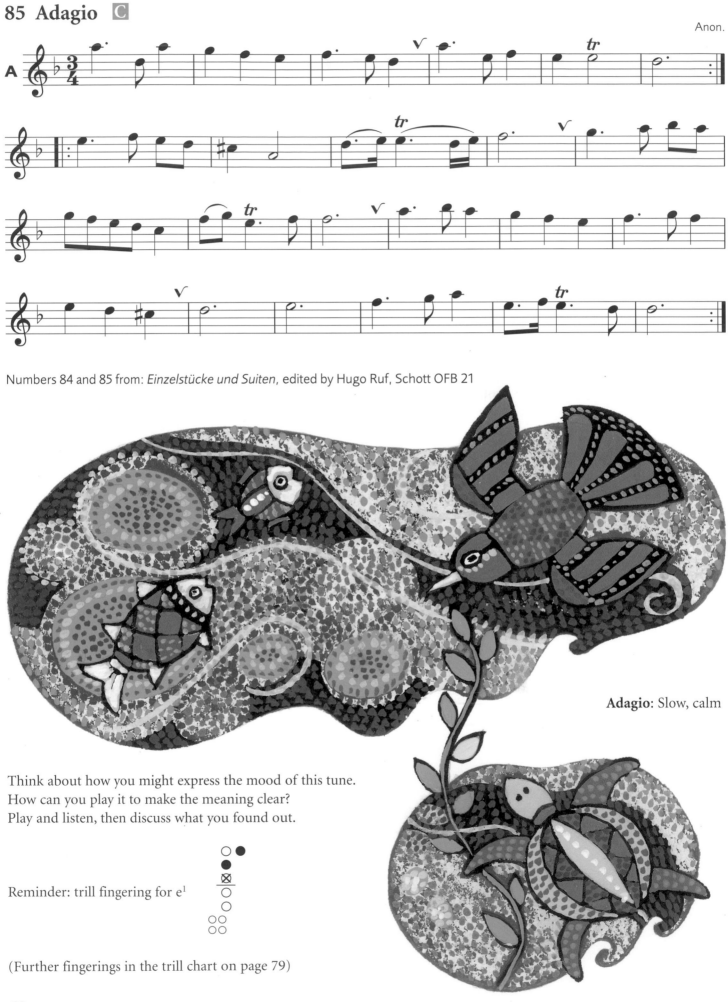

Numbers 84 and 85 from: *Einzelstücke und Suiten,* edited by Hugo Ruf, Schott OFB 21

Adagio: Slow, calm

Think about how you might express the mood of this tune.
How can you play it to make the meaning clear?
Play and listen, then discuss what you found out.

Reminder: trill fingering for e¹

(Further fingerings in the trill chart on page 79)

86 High-spirited

G. Engel

shake

T There are trios and quartets to play on pages 10–11 of the **Tune Book**.

Breathing exercises C

Stand with your weight equally divided between both feet and place your hands around your waist with fingers to the front and thumbs to the back. Your shoulders are 'heavy' and your arms hang bent at your hips.
Now breathe in with two sharp intakes of air (can you feel the two movements with your hands?), hold the air for one beat and then push the air out again with two short puffs. Are you out of air? If not, give one final puff to blow out the rest.

When you are completely out of air begin the cycle again:
breath in: 1. through your open mouth
              2. through your nose
Can you feel a difference?
What do you notice when you breathe out?

Pick up your instrument and repeat the exercise on the note g:
Breathe in as above and then blow   1. a wave-note (one beat = one wave)
                                      2. a straight note

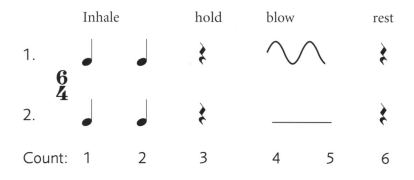

87 Long journey

G. Heyens

rit.

The bar lines have been left out of this piece so that you can concentrate on the phrasing.
Try to play each of the phrases legato.

T For more pieces with long legato phrases play Bicinium I and II, **Tune Book** pages 29–30.

High D

A   d²

Fingering and tone exercise for d² [C]

Ensure that you are holding your recorder correctly (supported by your thumb and lower lip).
Your left thumb must be able to move freely.
Whilst playing a long d² move your left thumb around on its hole until the note is free of whistling and breathiness
and only a beautiful clear high d sounds. Try to remember the exact position of your thumb on the hole.

your thumb searches…

…your thumb finds the right position

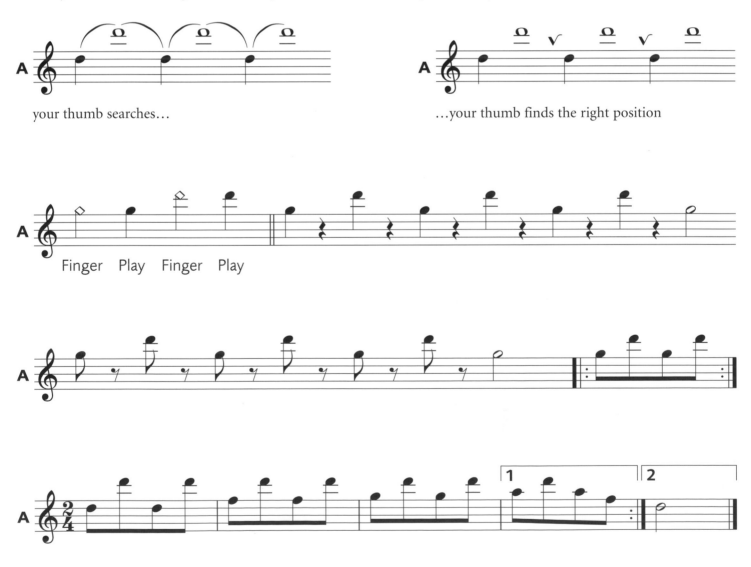

Finger   Play   Finger   Play

64

88 Scale exercise

What key are these two exercises in?

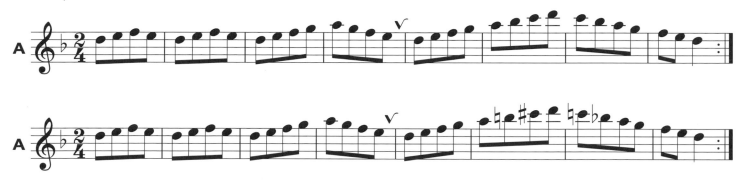

Play the scale exercises from memory.

T In the **Tune Book** (p. 15) 'Morning Walk' by A. Gretchaninoff uses high d while
Bassedance 'Bernadine' (p. 16) is in the key of d minor.

Three Wintery Songs C

89

Melody: 16th cent.
Text: P. C. B.

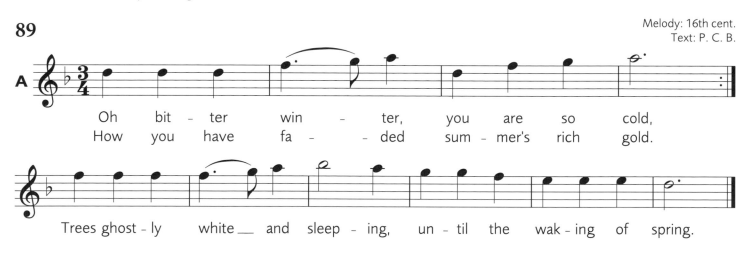

Oh   bit – ter   win –   ter,   you   are   so   cold,
How   you   have   fa –   – ded   sum – mer's   rich   gold.

Trees ghost – ly   white __ and   sleep – ing,   un – til   the   wak – ing   of   spring.

90

M. Praetorius, 1610
English translation: P. C. B

My heart longs for the green of spring in dark and bit - ter times,
The weight of win - ter's snow bears hard up - on the for - est pines.

The sing - ing of the birds so sweet for months has not been heard, Ex - pelled by na-ture's

an - gry feet they force a - way the sum - mer treat; leave sil - ence, cold and hard.

91

Melody: Anon. 16th cent.
Words: P. C. B.

A - way cruel win - ter from this land, with frost and ice that bites the

hand. All praise now for the warmth and light that drives a - way cold win-ter's night.

Xylophone

Percussion

Accompaniment:

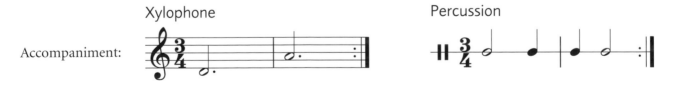

C

Talk about the character of these pieces. What was winter like for people in the old days?
How can we express this through music?

92 Mango walk

Trad. West Indian

My bro-ther did-a tell me that you go man-go walk, you

go man-go walk, you go man-go walk. My bro-ther did-a tell me that you

go man-go walk and steal all the num-ber 'le-ven.

Now tell me Joe, do tell me for true, do tell me for true, do tell me, that

you don't go to no man-go walk and steal all the num-ber

'le-ven. My bro-ther did-a tell me that you go man-go walk, you

go man-go walk, you go man-go walk. My bro-ther did-a tell me that you

go man-go walk and steal all the num-ber 'le-ven.

T Tune Book pages 18–20

Listen - Play - Improvise

Echo game C

Before beginning this echo game have a look again at the last improvisation exercises on page 53.

Our interval this time is:

Write out your own improvised melodies:

Count: 1 2 3 4 1 2 3 4

93 Les Bouffons (the fools)

Pièrre Phalèse
(1510–1573)

A

Ornamented
version

Play 'Les Bouffons' in a silly, lively and boisterous way. Play it from memory. Make up your own ornaments.

94 William of Nassau

At the beginning of Modo 2 we have highlighted the main notes from the original tune.
Can you complete this for the remainder of the piece?

Jacob van Eyck
(1590–1657)

95 Courante

Add your own ornaments to this courante.

Michael Praetorius
(1571–1621)

From: *50 Tanzweisen der Renaissance*, Schott ED 12266

Courante: a fast 'running' dance
          in triple time

96 Passepied

Leopold Mozart
(1719–1787)

From: *Solobuch für Altblockflöte.* Pieces from the 17th and 18th centuries, Schott ED 4796

Passepied: A lively country dance, which became popular
at the court of Louis XIV of France.

97 A canao virou (the canoe capsized!)

Brazilian folk song
Setting: G. Engel

The Magic Note

(An intonation exercise using the difference tone)

No-one plays it but despite that you can hear a third note!
Play two soprano recorders exactly in tune:

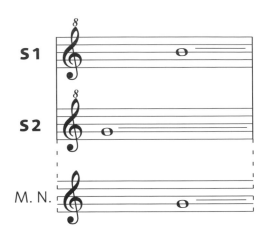

Be patient, you may not be able to hear the magic note straight away. It may be that you are slightly out of tune. If necessary, alter your breath pressure a little to get the intonation just right.
The magic note from the interval g–b is our new note on the alto recorder!

Low g

g¹

98 Finger exercise

G. H.

First play through this exercise without sounding the notes, but striking them audibly with your fingers.

72

99 Little dance

G. Engel

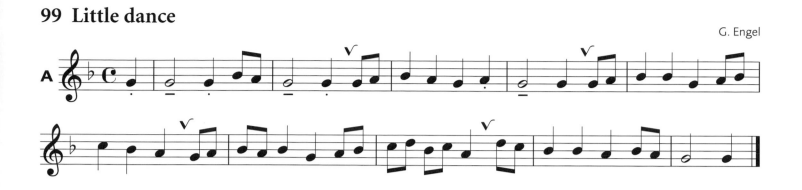

100 Arpeggio exercise

101 A jig

P. C. B.

102 Villageoise

J. B. de Boismortier
(1682–1765)

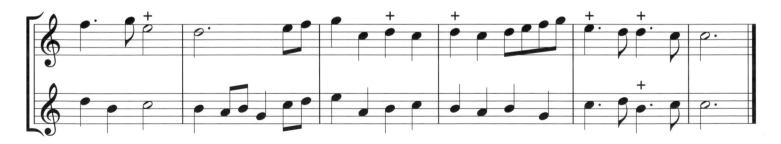

From: Boismortier, *6 leichte Duette* (6 easy duets), Schott OFB 6

T There are more duets in the **Tune Book**, page 21.

Villageoise: A rustic tune

103 Little Rondo

From an old duet book ca. 1740

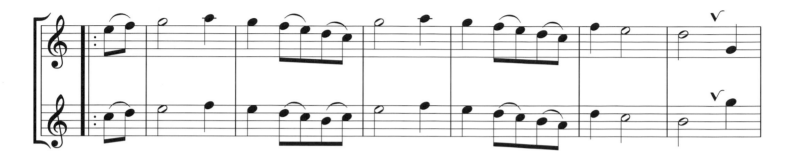

From: *Little Duets by Old Masters*, Vol. 1, Schott ED 4373

Warm-up exercises for 'The Cat and the Mouse' C

Finger numbers are shown in the Fingering Chart, page 80.

104 The Cat and the Mouse C

G. Heyens

A cat walks through the garden,   the mouse

The mouse, unaware, darts around.

hears its steps!   The cat stalks, - - - gets ready to pounce and grabs the mouse.

The mouse is in danger,   where is the mouse hole? The mouse shakes with fear,

She growls greedily, and throws the mouse in the air.   The cat walks around the garden.
(repeat several times)

whimpers, cries...   p ———— ff   ... and escapes!

*) Fingering for 'grabs the mouse'

**) for 'throws it up', cover the labium with your right hand whilst fingering a c with your left hand.

Index of Tunes, Songs and Games

Trill fingerings

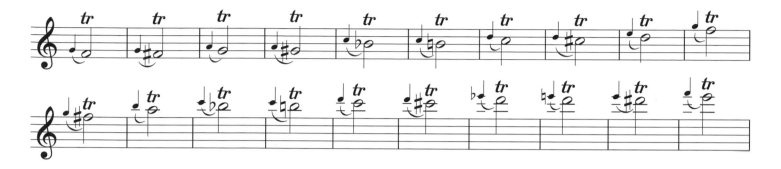

All of the above trills can easily be played using normal fingerings.

For the following trills alternative fingerings are used which make the trills easier to perform. In some cases only a small finger movement is necessary.

The chart shows the fingering for the upper note of the trill (small note) - the main note sounds when the hole ⊗ is covered and the holes in brackets ( ) uncovered. The finger holes in brackets remain open through the trill. They are only closed when playing the beginning note of the trill.

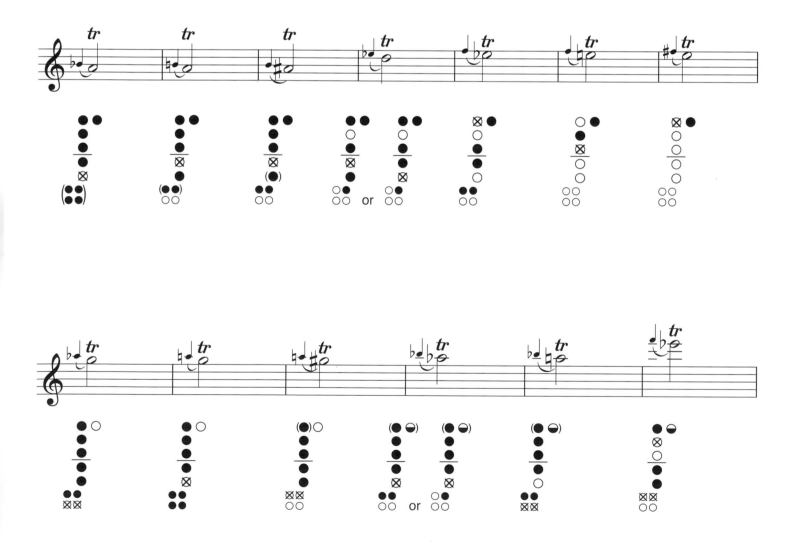

Fingering chart

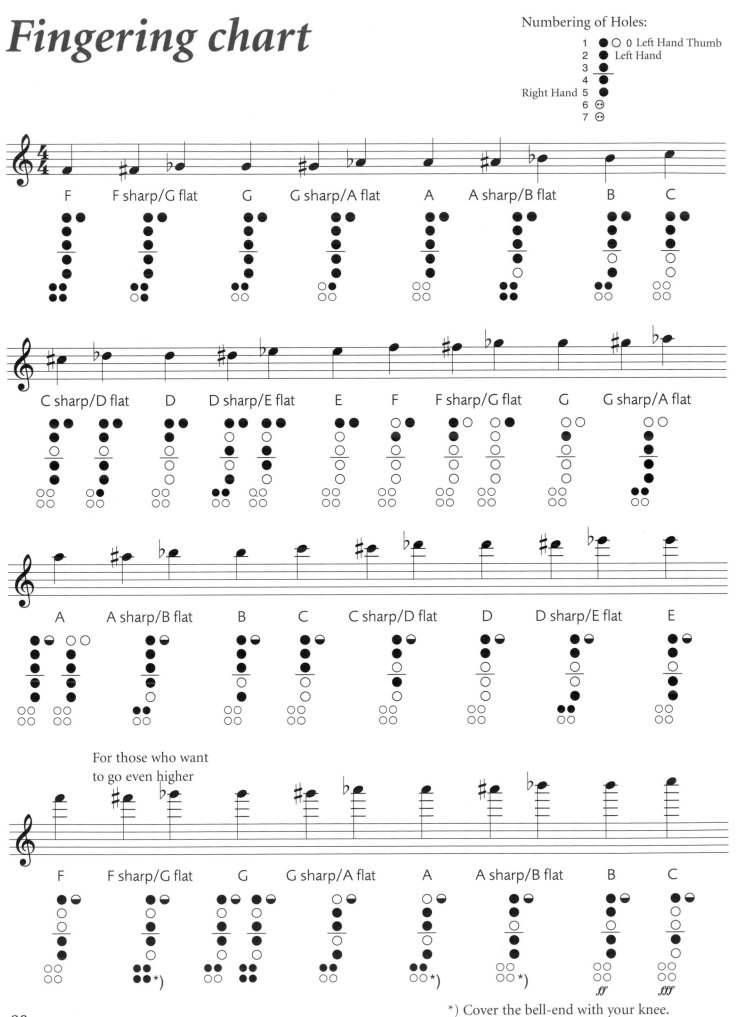

*) Cover the bell-end with your knee.
Sometimes this hole is given the number 8.